>>> **e-guidelines** 3

Developing
e-learning materials

Applying user-centred design

Shubhanna Hussain

niace

promoting adult learning

371.334

ⓝiace

T30576

©2005 National Institute of Adult Continuing Education
(England and Wales)
21 De Montfort Street
Leicester
LE1 7GE

Company registration no. 2603322
Charity registration no. 1002775

NIACE has a broad remit to promote lifelong learning opportunities
for adults. NIACE works to develop increased participation in
education and training, particularly for those who do not have easy
access because of class, gender, age, race, language and culture,
learning difficulties or disabilities, or insufficient financial resources.

You can find NIACE online at **www.niace.org.uk**

Cataloguing in Publication Data
A CIP record of this title is available from the British Library

Designed and typeset by Patrick Armstrong, Book Production
Services, London

Printed and bound in the UK by Latimer Trend
ISBN: 1 86201 226 1

Contents

Introduction

An ever-increasing number of tutors and curriculum leaders in adult and community learning (ACL) are developing e-learning resources for their own use and to share with colleagues. The term e-learning resource can include electronic worksheets, interactive learning materials (e.g. CD-ROMs or websites with learning resources) online discussions (e.g. real-time chat or email discussions), or virtual learning environments.

During 2003–2004, several projects, such as TACL (Tools for Adult and Community Learning) and TrEACL (Technology to Enhance Adult and Community Learning), were initiated to encourage tutors in adult and community learning to develop their own e-learning resources. These initiatives, funded in England by the Learning and Skills Council, were widely welcomed by tutors in ACL.

This book will guide you through a simple, user-centred approach to the design of e-learning resources, and will provide examples and guidelines to help you produce e-learning resources that meet the needs of your learners. It will suggest ways in which established practices of materials development can be adapted by tutors and curriculum leaders to create e-learning materials in ACL. The projects describes vary greatly in scale, from modest enterprises where individual tutors use simple, free or low-cost software to produce small amounts of material to much larger projects which have had significant funding. The principles it lays down can be applied to any materials-development process, but they will need to be interpreted in a manner appropriate to the scale of the project.

Acknowledgements

Thanks to the projects and individuals who provided case-studies for this book, in particular: Graham Wroe; Friends Centre, Brighton; Knowsley Local Education Authority; Ideogram; Digital Fife.

I would also thank Alastair Clark for reading earlier drafts and providing helpful feedback and advice.

1

The benefits of creating
e-learning resources

The creation of e-learning resources from scratch requires the use of authoring tools and staff time – both to learn how to use the tools and, subsequently, to create the resources. This means your organisation will probably require a reasonable amount of funding. Buying ready-to-use e-learning resources may seem like a cheaper alternative: the only real cost involved is the initial purchase of the e-learning resource.

One of the criticisms of ready-to-use e-learning resources is that very few of them are intended for an adult audience. By creating your own materials you will be able to tailor the content and the media used to the needs of your learners. You will also be able to contextualise the content with appropriate references, images and local accents.

Everybody has a preferred way of learning – some learn better through visual media or by listening to audio clips rather than by using text-based material. Developing your own resources will allow you to cater to the individual learning needs of your learners. Also, mastering the techniques needed to create e-learning resources will enable you to adapt materials as your learners progress through the course.

Developing your own e-learning resources will allow you and your colleagues to overcome many of the problems generally associated with ready-to-use e-learning resources. Hence, the longer-term benefits of creating in-house e-learning resources will often far outweigh the initial costs involved in buying authoring software and devoting staff time to the making of the resources.

2

▬

Usability

In the context of e-learning resources, usability is a measure of how easy it is for your learners and tutors to understand and make sense of the 'user interface'. Failure to consider usability issues when designing e-learning resources can lead to the production of materials that your tutors or learners find difficult to use. If e-learning resources are not user-friendly then your learners will rapidly become frustrated, especially those who are new to information technology. Badly designed e-learning resources can reduce motivation and possibly affect retention.

The usability issues you should bear in mind are:

> **Learnability**
  How easy is it for your tutors and learners to learn how to use the e-learning resources?

> **Attitude**
  Do your tutors and learners enjoy using the e-learning resources? Do they find them user-friendly?

> **Flexibility**
  Is it easy to adapt the resources to meet the needs of learners with different ICT or learning abilities?

> **Effectiveness**
  Does the resource meet the purpose for which it was designed – i.e. does it meet the learning objectives of the course?

In order to have a better understanding of how your tutors and learners will interact with the interface of an e-learning resource, it is useful to have some knowledge of the *Theory of Action* (see Norman, 1988, *The Design of Everyday Things*).

Generally, a person carrying out a task begins with a goal in mind. They then take action to achieve this goal – this is known as the *execution stage*. They also want some way of checking that their goal was achieved through the action that they took– this is known as the *evaluation stage*.

Difficulties that learners experience when trying to use e-learning resources are often due to:

> **Gulf of execution** – learners may have a goal or task in mind but do not know how to achieve that goal or task using the e-learning resource.

> **Gulf of evaluation** – the learner may commence a task using the e-learning resource, but then has no way of telling whether the task has been completed satisfactorily – i.e. there is no feedback.

In order to bridge these gulfs, and to ensure that the e-learning resources are usable, you should have a clear understanding of what your learners will want from the e-learning resource and what approaches and methods they will respond to best. Making no attempt to find out any of this may result in the production of an e-learning resource that no-one wants or knows how to use.

Photo: Nick Hayes

The best way to ensure that usability issues are taken into consideration is by adopting a user-centred approach to designing e-learning resources. The next chapter will go into greater detail about this approach, but essentially, a user-centred approach will require you to:

> keep focused on why you are designing the e-learning resource;
> find out as much as you can about your potential users (the tutor and learners) and keep them in mind as you design the resource;
> pay attention to design and accessibility guidelines;
> use an iterative design process by developing paper prototypes or low-technology versions of your e-learning resource and testing them out;
> evaluate the resource against your initial aims and objectives throughout the design process.

3

What is user-centred design?

The creation and development of one or a set of e-learning resources should be regarded as a significant, formal project, with time-scales and budgets allocated to each stage of the process. It is important to define clearly all of the processes that need to happen before, during and after the resources have been developed. The size of the project will vary according to the staff time and budget available and the amount of material to be created, but whatever the scale the same processes can be applied.

User-centred design methodology is a simple and easy-to-understand model which incorporates all of these processes. It is not a new concept: in fact, many tutors are probably applying aspects of user-centred design when designing their e-learning resources without realising it. The user-centred model is commonly associated with the design of software and websites in the commercial sector, but it can easily be adapted to working with limited resources. Following a user-centred methodology ensures that the design of your e-learning resources is driven by your users' needs and not by the technology. It also addresses issues of quality, usability and evaluation by ensuring that your users are considered, and often involved, at every stage of the development process.

There are variations of the user-centred model, but the common factor in all of them is that they are 'iterative'. This means that the design–development cycle is repeated until a final resource is developed that your users are happy with.

Shown on pages 6–7 is an example of a user-centred model which would be useful for developing e-learning resources in ACL.

Stage 1: Requirements

Requirements of your organisation

Identify key stakeholders

Conduct feasibility study

User requirements

Requirements of learners

Requirements of tutors

Stage 2: Planning

Identify the learning objectives for the course and decide on the learning activities / content you want the resource to cover

Follow principle of learning theory

Take usability issues into consideration

Stage 3: Design–development

Design a prototype
e-learning resource

Implement changes
to prototype

Test the prototype
with users

This design – evaluate – redesign process continues until users are satisfied that the
design meets their needs.

Then, develop a fully functional
version of the e-learning resource
using appropriate design tools

Stage 4: Implementation

Provide training and
support to tutors and
learners using the e-
learning resource for the
first time

Use and evaluate your e-
learning resources with
tutors and learners

Finally, keep a record
of all the processes
and the results of any
evaluations for future
developments to the
resource

User-centred model for developing e-learning resources

The user-centred model has four main stages

> requirements
> planning
> design and development
> implementation.

There is an element of evaluation built into each stage of the process to ensure the usability of the e-learning resources.

By carrying out some form of evaluation throughout the development cycle you can ensure that a working and user-friendly version of your e-learning resource is available by the project deadline. It is important also to plan in the time to make any changes to the resource as a result of feedback from evaluations. Evaluations are a waste of time and resources if the recommended changes are not implemented in the final product. Ongoing evaluations take time, but the investment in this time is well worth while, as changes to a prototype are much easier to achieve than changes to a final, fully working version.

The case study on pages 9, 10 and 11 shows how the user-centered model might be applied in practice.

The succeeding chapters will look at each of the four stages in the user-centred design model in more detail and highlight the evaluation processes which should take place.

Improve your Polish –
A case study

An example of how user-centred design could be applied to the production of materials to support a Polish-language class.

The development team was made up of three members of staff who had undertaken training in e-learning, and one learner. The developers were: a tutor of Polish, a tutor of Spanish who was learning Polish herself, and the curriculum coordinator for modern foreign languages, who joined in the development team meetings and undertook a small amount of the material production.

Stage 1: Requirements (see chapters 4 and 5)

Requirements of the organisation (April)
The development group conducted a feasibility study and established that the Polish class, which is based in a secondary school, could access the Internet by moving into a dedicated IT suite and could occasionally book laptops without Internet access to use in their normal classroom. They decided that production on CD-ROM would give more flexibility than a web-based resource. The organisation's e-learning strategy supported this approach.

Identifying user requirements (April)
The tutors adapted existing course evaluation sheets during the summer term of year 1 to establish.

1 which sectors of the curriculum were proving challenging for learners, and for which sectors the introduction of e-learning materials would add significant value to the course;
2 learners' levels of IT skills.

9

The Polish tutor provided a scheme of work for year 2 indicating the areas where previous years' learners had been found to need additional support.

The tutors also organised a half-day workshop where they invited other modern language tutors to look at the current resources available and to discuss their experiences of using e-learning resources.

Stage 2: Planning (see chapter 6)

In May, the development group looked carefully at the results of the evaluation, the tutors' comments and their survey of the location. The group made a list of materials that they planned to produce and decided to produce the work using software that transfers word-processed documents to web pages, and to employ some simple quiz software. This route was chosen to reduce costs and training time for the developers.

The group decided to adapt Gagné's model of instructional design for their work (see p 26). As their materials would be largely used in blended leaning situations they did not feel they needed to stick rigidly to all nine events of Gagné's model, as some of these would be covered in face-to-face work by the tutor.

Stage 3: Design and development (see chapter 7)

This phase took place between June and August.

The Polish tutor designed the first draft of the e-learning resource on paper. This was tested initially with the two other members of the team using a co-operative evaluation approach. Following a few amendments, an electronic version of the material was produced.

A test group was established made up of two learners of Polish, one French tutor and one German tutor. This group then used a heuristic evaluation approach (see Glossary p 47) to evaluate the interface of the resource against a set of usability guidelines.

The development team listened carefully to the comments and realised that there were improvements needed to the resource's navigation procedures and systems. They made the changes to the resource and invited back the test group, who offered feedback. One of the pieces of feedback was that all of the Polish audio was spoken by the tutor, which learners felt was too familiar. As a result, three members, male and female, of a nearby Polish club were invited to re-record the clips.

Another piece of feedback was that learners found it motivating to see photographs of genuine Polish products, including Polish labels and advertisements, but the illustrations of public buildings used in the resource were, in fact, examples taken locally. As a result, the centre secretary, who was due to go for city break to Krakow, was asked to help. She agreed to take the photographs required and, as a bonus, she also brought back a short video of a waiter saying 'well done' in Polish.

Stage 4: Implementation (see chapter 8)

Implementation in September was relatively easy as the Polish tutor was familiar with the materials. However, he did need to familiarise himself with the laptops and the IT suite and to make sure that he had sufficient copies of the resource on CD ROM. He found that some of the CD ROM drives in the IT suite were disabled so he also loaded the resource on to the school network.

The elements of the resource were introduced throughout the year at the rate of about one per month. After each new element was used, the learners were asked for feedback on a very simple evaluation sheet.

Follow up

The resource was displayed at the language tutors' training day in December, and Spanish and Italian tutors expressed interest in adapting the material for their languages. They were able to use all the existing documentation for the Polish e-learning resource to inform their work.

4

Requirements of the organisation

Before you begin designing your e-learning resources, it is important that you have the commitment of key stakeholders.

Key stakeholders are anyone who will be affected by the introduction of e-learning resources. In most cases this is likely to be:

> the learners;
> tutors involved in designing and delivering the learning;
> staff and management who will be financing the resources;
> anyone else within the organisation with a vested interest in the development of e-learning resources, e.g. IT support staff.

It is important to engage with these groups, as each of them will have different needs. For example, your learners will be looking for resources that will make their subjects more interesting; your tutors will be looking for resources that are easy to create and meet the needs of their courses; and funders or managers will be looking for resources that provide best value for money.

The development of e-learning resources should be carefully project-managed, and deadlines should be set for each stage of the process. A small working group made up of stakeholders should aim to meet at key milestone stages of the project to ensure that it is running to time and budget.

Photo: Nick Hayes

All stakeholders need to be convinced that developing e-learning materials meets the needs of both the organisation and the learners.

Projects that have been successful in developing their own e-learning resources stressed the importance of having enthusiastic staff who could see the potential of developing their own e-learning resources.

Organising e-learning staff development days for your tutors is one way of introducing them to software and technologies for developing e-learning resources. This exposure to different e-learning resources may encourage them to make use of such resources in their own courses.

The very process of engaging tutors is often enough to secure their support. If, however, full support is not forthcoming then at least the process can help to identify where the resistance lies and how best to address it.

Friends Centre, Brighton

The Friends Centre in Brighton wanted to enhance teaching and learning in their ESOL programme by enabling tutors to make better use of ICT resources and e-learning approaches. Eight ESOL tutors took part in training to learn how to use *Hot Potatoes* to create crosswords, gap-fill exercises and word-matches. The tutors created portfolios of practical examples that were made available to other tutors.

Through a series of staff development workshops, the ESOL tutors were able to share their resources with other Friends Centre tutors and ESOL tutors across Brighton.

These games and puzzles seem to be an entertaining, educational and non-threatening approach – tutor (Friends Centre).

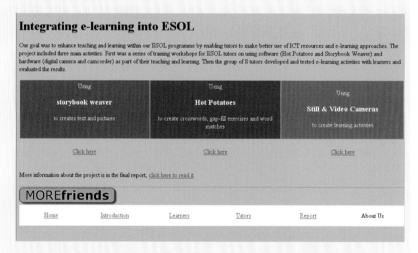

The Friends Website, which contains examples of e-learning resources created by their tutors. (www.morefriends.org.uk)

Making the choice to develop your own e-learning resources requires commitment not only from the tutors developing and delivering the learning but also from the management.

A number of TACL-funded organisations carried out small-scale pilot schemes and developed e-learning resources in a subject area where the staff were enthusiastic and confident about designing their own e-learning resources. This worked particularly well for organisations that were only just beginning to take their first tentative steps into e-learning. The positive experiences of staff who participated in these pilots was often enough to convince senior managers of the benefits of developing e-learning resources in other subject areas.

Feasibility study

When setting out to develop e-learning resources it is important to know what is already available and what is required in the organisation. Conducting a feasibility study is a good way of identifying these environmental constraints. For example:

> What level of infrastructure exists at your learning locations?
> How will the resource development be funded?

See Polish case study (page 9).

The type and level of infrastructure available in the organisation where you will be delivering the learning will have an impact on the type of e-learning resources you design. Key infrastructure considerations are connectivity and hardware availability. In general, you must assess whether the technical infrastructure currently available in your organisation and in the locations where you will be delivering the learning can handle the e-learning resources you want to implement.

You need to decide how your learners will access the e-learning resources that you develop, and whether Internet access is required. Some of the most common approaches to access e-learning resources are:

> locally on stand-alone PCs or laptops;
> through a network within the learning centre / school or college where learning is delivered;
> using a CD-ROM;
> on a learning platform;
> via the World Wide Web.

Each of these approaches has its own benefits and pitfalls that you need to be aware of before making a decision about how your e-learning resources will be accessed. For example, if you are using school or college locations to deliver your learning, you may find that there are restrictions on what you can load on to the computers locally or on to the network.

If you require Internet access for your e-learning resources then you need the answers to two important questions:

> Is there Internet access at the location you will be delivering e-learning?
> Is the bandwidth at the location adequate for web-based e-learning resources?

If your e-learning resources require access to high-resolution images, audio, video and multimedia from the Internet, then remember that these can take a long time to download, especially if you are using a dial-up connection. Many dial-up connections can be very slow, which will not only adversely affect the teaching and learning process but may also frustrate learners who have not had much experience of using the Internet.

If upgrading your bandwidth is not feasible you should consider alternative resources such as a CD-ROM. However, remember that you will need to ensure that your learners can access a CD-ROM: don't assume that all PCs or laptops at your learning locations come with CD-ROM drives.

If your e-learning resources require plug-ins for audio, video, animations or multimedia ensure that these are available on the computers or laptops at your learning locations. Again, you may find that there are restrictions on the types of software you can download on to computers in certain learning locations.

The full cost of designing and developing effective e-learning resources needs to be recognised. This will include the initial costs of buying the authoring tools, the cost of buying any additional equipment, as well as staff time to learn how to use the tools, and then the time taken to create the resources and test them with users. Depending on what is already available within the organisation in terms of staff skills and infrastructure you may need to consider spending money on some or all of the following:

> authoring tools (and licences);
> additional hardware to enable learners to use e-learning resources (for example, additional laptops, digital cameras etc.);
> staff time to create e-learning resources and to train other staff members to use the authoring tools;
> developers to create the e-learning resources (if the job is outsourced);
> staff time to evaluate e-learning resources with users and analyse the feedback.

Budget considerations are likely to have an impact on the decisions that are made with regards to type of authoring tools to buy and the amount of staff time allowed to create the resources.

There is a lot of free software available to create simple e-learning resources, for instance *Hot Potatoes*. However, if you want to create something more sophisticated then you may need to invest in a relatively costly product like *Macromedia Authorware*. Again, you need to think about whether this will be a justifiable investment. Costs can be cut by joining with neighbouring organisations to share e-learning resources, authoring tools and staff expertise. Also, if you do not have any IT expertise within your organisation then it may be worthwhile considering a partnership with local e-learning developers. Creating partnerships with developers can help organisations that do not have the resources to train staff in using authoring tools.

5
Requirements of users

The requirements stage is an essential part of the user-centred model. Spending time and effort at this stage to understand who your users are and what they want from an e-learning resource will ensure that the materials you develop meet their requirements.

Requirements of learners

Knowing what motivates your learners or why they have chosen to do your course will provide you with some useful information about the type of resources that may interest them. The more that tutors know about their learners' needs and motivation the better the resources they will create.

Most tutors will appreciate that learners learn in different ways, and so e-learning resources which work with one group of learners may not necessarily work with another. For example, some learners may respond better to graphics and animation whereas others may prefer the use of text and written narrative, or audio material, to understand concepts and relationships. In practice, good learning materials should deliver the learning in a variety of ways to suit a range of learning styles.

Learners will also differ in the amount of knowledge or experience they have with ICT. This will also have an impact on the level or type of e-learning resource that will be most effective.

The ICT skills and knowledge of your learners will affect the type of e-learning resources you develop. There are a number of different methods to assess the ICT abilities of your learners. For instance, you can survey your group of learners using a brief questionnaire to find out how they rate their computer skills. However this method can be problematic: learners may over- or under-estimate their ability to use certain software or technologies.

Another method is to observe a group of your learners as they work through existing e-learning resources. Make a note of what they prefer or have difficulties with. For example, does having audio or video clips enhance their learning or is it just a hindrance? Are there particular colours or fonts which they find difficult to read on screen? Do they prefer text-based or activity-based resources? Do they have difficulties using the mouse?

Photo: Nick Hayes

The Polish case study on page 9 provides an example of how tutors can identify learners' requirements.

Requirements of tutors

It is important to remember that other tutors will also be using these resources to teach, so their needs and requirements should also be taken into consideration when designing the resources.

Speak to tutors across the different curriculum areas to find out the best ways in which e-learning resources could support their work. If other tutors have used e-learning resources before, find out what their experiences have been and what changes, if any, they would like to see in a new e-learning resource.

The knowledge and understanding of ICT that the teaching staff in your organisation have will impact on the type of e-learning resources that you develop.

If the tutors have a basic understanding of ICT, and can use search engines on the World Wide Web to find e-learning resources and download documents from web pages, then they will be able to use these skills to create webquests, a really simple but effective tool to use with learners. (For more on webquests, see *Online Resources in the Classroom* (Clarke and Hesse, 2004).)

Tutors who have an intermediate understanding of ICT will be able to create simple exercises using applications such as Word and PowerPoint. They may also be able to add audio or visual clips to their e-learning resources if they feel that this is appropriate to the learning objectives.

Tutors with advanced understanding of ICT may feel confident about using authoring tools such as *Hot Potatoes*, *CourseGenie* or *Macromedia* Authorware. These can be used to create some simple but effective e-learning resources.

As well as having the necessary ICT skills and knowledge, it is also important that tutors have the confidence to develop e-learning resources that can be used with their learners. If the tutors have never created any form of e-learning resource then it is best to start at the most basic level: for example, by developing simple webquests, and then building on this.

Webquests

Webquests are inquiry-oriented activities in which some or all of the information that learners interact with comes from resources on the Internet. The ACLearn website (www.aclearn.net) provides a number of webquest templates which can be used to create some simple webquests for your learners.

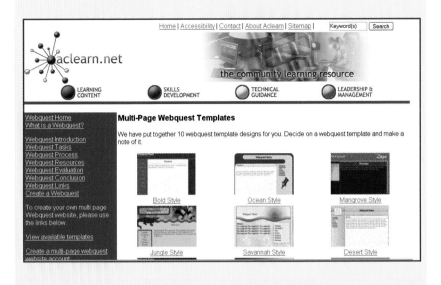

6

Planning the e-learning resource

Knowing who your potential users are and conducting a feasibility study informs you of the needs of your learners and tutors as well as making you aware of what you have in terms of staff skills, infrastructure and funds. The next stage is to apply this information to the planning of your e-learning resources.

All e-learning resources should:

> be appropriate to the learning goals and objectives of the course;
> follow principles of instructional design;
> take into consideration usability issues.

Learners will ultimately judge your course on the quality of the content. Making use of ICT and e-learning resources may get the learners interested in a subject, but you will need good-quality content to ensure that you then retain these learners.

Learning objectives

Before you begin designing an e-learning resource, you should be clear about its purpose and how it would fit into the learning objectives of the course being taught.

The purpose of an e-learning resource can be:

> to teach a subject in an interactive way;

> to reinforce a piece of learning;

> to help develop or learn new skills;

> to provide formative or summative assessment.

It is not usually appropriate to teach an entire lesson using an e-learning resource. For example, learners in fitness, arts and crafts classes would prefer to spend the majority of their time in class, actively engaged in the core course activities rather than sitting at computers. In these situations, e-learning resources such as interactive quizzes or worksheets can be used to reinforce or extend topics that have been learnt in the classroom.

If you intend to develop a resource to teach a large part of the course, for example learning a language, then you may consider developing resources which make use of learning objects. Learning objects are small stand-alone 'chunks' of information designed to be easily reused to meet the needs of different learners. The National Learning Network (NLN) defines learning objects as short episodes or units of learning lasting around 10–20 minutes and which comprise all of the following three elements:

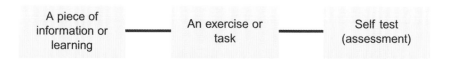

One of the benefits of developing learning objects is that they have the potential to be 'repurposed' and used across different subject areas and with different groups of learners. Developing e-learning resources that can be repurposed makes the development process much more efficient, as it cuts down on the time needed to create and design new materials from scratch.

Once you have a clear idea of the type of e-learning resource you would like to create, a decision needs to be made about whether you are going to create the resources yourself or outsource the development work externally.

The benefit of outsourcing is that you get an e-learning resource which can look very professional and take a relatively short period of time to develop. However, you need to be careful that it does not deter tutors from attempting to develop their own resources, as they may feel that they cannot compete with standards set by a professional developer.

You also need to compare the costs of outsourcing and developing e-learning resources in-house. In-house development will require the purchase of authoring tools as well as paying for staff time to learn how to use the authoring tools and then develop the resources. However, paying for developers is not necessarily the cheaper alternative.

Also, bear in mind that the developers will not be content experts, so it is important that you provide them with clear instructional design and keep in regular contact, as a good working relationship will ensure that the e-learning resources meet the requirements of both the learners and the tutors.

If you make the decision to develop your own resources and you know exactly what you need in terms of design tools then you can often find free or low-cost authoring tools, for example *Hot Potatoes*, *Web Quiz*, *Course Genie*, or *Acce-Lerator*.

Your choice of authoring tools will ultimately depend on:

> your budget;
> the ICT skills of your tutor staff;
> the time available to learn how to use the software if it is new to the organisation.

Knowsley LEA and Ideogram

Revise your Spanish is a multimedia application developed by Knowsley LEA in partnership with Ideogram. The CD-ROM helps students learn Spanish and also focuses on basic skills, ICT and study skills. The project was successful because of the close working partnership between the LEA and the developers, who supplied and updated the CD for evaluation every two to four weeks. The updates were tested by the tutors who wrote the content. This regular testing enabled content changes such as text edits and corrections, improvement to navigation interface and interactive content improvement. This all helped to make the *Revise your Spanish* more accessible and enhanced the learning experience for the user.

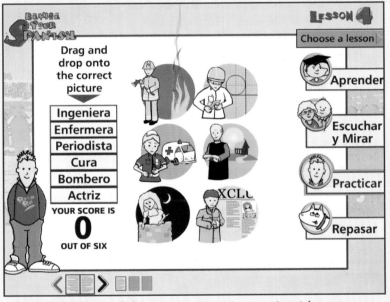

Screenshot of drag and drop exercise in Revise your Spanish

Instructional design

Instructional design is a way of organising e-learning resources to ensure that learners achieve the established learning outcomes.

There are several instructional design models. Gagne's 1987 model known as the *nine events of instruction*, has been very influential.

A blind student testing an e-learning resource using JAWS software.
Photo: Nick Hayes

Consider including accessibility awareness training for your developers. There is a number of organisations that can help you to do this, and provide you with useful advice on how to enhance the accessibility of your e-learning materials.

AbilityNet provides free information and advice, individual assessment of technology needs and the supply of assistive technology with free support. **www.abilitynet.co.uk**

ACLearn is a community learning resource website which provides information about the extension of the National Learning Network (NLN) to Adult and Community Learning (ACL). It also has some useful advice on accessibility.
www.aclearn.net/content/instructional-design/accessibility

BOBBY is a tool for Web authors to assess whether their pages are accessible for people with disabilities and also whether a web resource conforms to the W3C web-content accessibility guidelines.
www.bobby.watchfire.com

Browsealoud is software that will speech-enable your web site and help people with low literacy and reading skills, dyslexia, and learners whose first language is not English to navigate your resource. **www.browsealoud.com**

JAWS® for Windows is a popular screen-reader that works with your PC to provide access to software applications and the Internet. **www.freedomscientific.com/fs_products/software_jaws.asp**

Supernova is a reader magnifier, which enables magnification, speech, Braille, or all three, opening up access to Windows. **www.dolphincomputeraccess.com/products/supernova**

TechDis provides information and advice for technology related to disability and inclusion. It also has some useful resources on how to make learning accessible for your learners. **www.techdis.ac.uk/**

Visibone provides colour charts and links to other useful resources for designers looking to avoid problems for learners with colour blindness. **www.visibone.com/colorblind**

W3C (World Wide Web Consortium) is an international consortium of companies involved with the Internet and the Web. One of its aims is to ensure that Web content is universally accessible. It provides Web content accessibility guidelines through its Web Accessibility Initiative (WAI). **www.w3.org/wai**

Usability

As well as ensuring that resource content is pedagogically sound, tutors need to also be aware of the usability of their e-learning resources. The way that learners interact with the interface of the e-learning resource is as important as getting content right. Content will often dictate many of the features of the interface. Nevertheless, navigating through e-learning resources should be made simple for learners so that they can concentrate on content and learning experience. A badly designed interface will leave the learner feeling confused or frustrated; it may even result in learners dropping out of the course.

There is a number of usability guidelines for websites and software that can easily be adapted for use with e-learning resources, for example Nielsen's heuristics (Nielsen, 1994). The following checklist is based on Neilsen's ideas. It can be used to ensure that the interface of the e-learning resource meets the usability criteria mentioned in chapter 2 (learnability, effectiveness, flexibility and user attitude).

Usability guidelines

> **Keep learners informed** of any delays between screens. For example, there may be a delay if large images are being downloaded. Generally, if there is a delay of more than ten seconds, then learners will begin to lose interest and will want to start performing other tasks.

> **Use plain language** and ensure that the words, phrases or concepts used in the e-learning resource are familiar to the learners.

> **Provide learners with control and freedom** to undo any function on the screen which they may have chosen by mistake. Also, provide learners with a clearly marked 'exit' to allow them to leave and return to the same point in the lesson.

> **Be consistent in design and layout** and use conventional software standards: learners will be used to certain navigation buttons.

> **Prevent learners from making errors** by ensuring that the e-learning resource is carefully designed to prevent a problem from occurring in the first place.

> **Make use of recognition rather than recall** by ensuring that all objects, actions and options are visible on the screen: then the learner does not have to remember information when moving from one screen to the next.

> **Ensure flexibility and efficiency of use** by allowing learners to go to any part of the e-learning resource without having to move sequentially through each lesson. Ensure that the content is written for an interactive medium and is not just repackaged course notes. Break information into chunks and use links to connect the relevant chunks so that you can support different uses of your content.

> **Use minimalist design** and remember that any extra unit of information on a screen competes with the relevant units of information and can therefore be a distraction and a slow-down. Place the most important information where it is most likely to attract attention, pay attention to the font and colour choices, and ensure that you make good use of white space.

> **Help learners to recognise, diagnose, and recover from errors** by ensuring that any error messages offers a solution and is expressed in plain English. The error message should indicate precisely what the problem is and suggest a solution.

> **Provide help and documentation** by integrating help pages into the resource. There should be links from the main sections of the resource into specific help and vice versa. Help could even be fully integrated into each page so that learners never feel that assistance is too far away. Ensure that any user documentation produced is written in a clear and easy-to-understand manner, and that the information focuses on the learners' tasks and lists the steps to be carried out.

Digital Fife
Making e-learning resources accessible

Digital Fife have made the e-learning resources on their website accessible for learners with a visual impairment by ensuring that the material can be used with a screen-reader, and provides users with an easyview option to increase the text size and allows the user to view the page in black and white. **www.digitalfife.com**

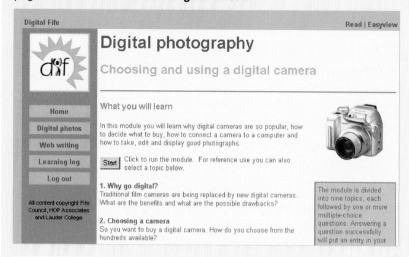

Digital Fife   Read | Easyview

Digital photography
Choosing and using a digital camera

What you will learn

In this module you will learn why digital cameras are so popular, how to decide what to buy, how to connect a camera to a computer and how to take, edit and display good photographs.

Start | Click to run the module. For reference use you can also select a topic below.

1. Why go digital?
Traditional film cameras are being replaced by new digital cameras. What are the benefits and what are the possible drawbacks?

2. Choosing a camera
So you want to buy a digital camera. How do you choose from the hundreds available?

The module is divided into nine topics, each followed by one or more multiple-choice questions. Answering a question successfully will put an entry in your

Home
Digital photos
Web writing
Learning log
Log out

All content copyright Fife Council, HOP Associates and Lauder College

---

Digital Fife   **Read | Normalview**

Digital photography

Choosing and using a digital camera

What you will learn

In this module you will learn why digital cameras are so popular, how to decide what to buy, how to connect a camera to a computer and how to take, edit and display good photographs.

Start | Click to run the module. For reference use you can also select a topic below.

1. Why go digital?

Home

Digital photos

Web writing

Learning log

Log out

The module is divided into nine topics, each

7
Design and development

The design and development stage is an iterative process that involves the following steps:

1   Create a prototype e-learning resource based on user requirements.
2   Test the prototype with learners and tutors and redesign the prototype based on user feedback. This test–redesign process should be repeated until the learners and tutors are happy with the design of the prototype.
3   Add functionality to the e-learning resource.
4   Evaluate the user interface of the fully functional resource with learners and tutors and change the interface in response to feedback from the learners and tutors.

Create a prototype

Creating a prototype of your e-learning resource is a fairly simple process. Based on user requirements, you can sketch the layout of your resource on paper, or use screenshots to give a more graphical representation of how your e-learning resource will look.

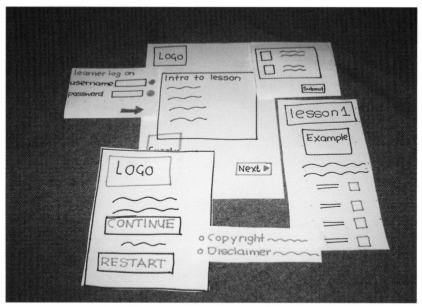

Paper prototypes of an e-learning resource Photo: Author

Prototypes can provide you with an insight into how your learners will use the resource and can also highlight issues that you may not have considered in the design of your resource. Prototypes are much easier and quicker to build than a fully functional version of your e-learning resource and will save you time and money in the long term, especially if significant changes have to be made.

Testing the prototype

Several evaluation techniques may be used to test prototypes with potential users. The 'simplified thinking aloud' technique, also known as co-operative evaluation, is one of the easiest and most effective methods. It requires potential users to carry out some typical tasks with the resource whilst 'thinking aloud'. Co-operative evaluation is a good method for identifying the discrepancies between what users expect to be able to do with an e-learning resource and what they can do in reality. This technique requires very little training or resources and can be carried out by evaluators without any specialised knowledge.

Two main categories of information are generated during co-operative evaluation: unexpected behaviour and user comments. Unexpected behaviour occurs when users do something that the designer did not intend them to do; user comments could be anything that the users say about the design or the performance of the e-learning resource.

Co-operative evaluations are particularly appropriate for the early prototyping stages of design, but are also useful for later evaluation purposes as well.

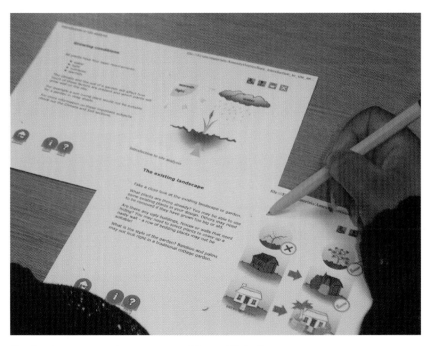

Evaluating a screenshot prototype. Photo: Nick Hayes

Carrying out a co-operative evaluation

1. Create a list of typical tasks that you would expect users to be able to do with the e-learning resource. The number of set tasks should be kept to a minimum to allow users some freedom to move around the resource. However, the tasks need to be reasonably specific to test whether the processes for carrying out the task are in place.

2. Recruit potential users, e.g. learners and teaching staff: between three and five users is usually sufficient. Collecting feedback from one user can give a considerable amount of insight; testing a second user will show some of the same problems as the first but will highlight some new problems; a third user will show many of the problems already found by the first two, but will generate a smaller amount of new information. Diminishing returns have set in: the more users added, the less that is learned each time.

3. Ask the users to 'think aloud' as they work through each of the tasks in turn. If it is relevant, you may also want to time how long it takes to complete each task. These tasks can be carried out on paper prototypes or on the screen versions of the e-learning resource.

4. Take notes and prompt the user as they work through the tasks. An audio recorder can be used to supplement notes. The record should provide a good insight into how the users feel about the resource.

5. Debrief the users and take note of all the comments they make about the resource.

This is an extract from a co-operative evaluation carried out with a learner whose task was to find a dressmaking course in his area.

Evaluator: can you find what courses there are for dressmaking in Leicester?

Learner clicks on 'find a course in your area', which takes him to a new screen. He spends a few moments reading the screen.

Learner: I expected to find something a lot less complicated than this. I thought I would find a screen which asked you 'what's your postcode' etc rather than the page that I've ended up with. There is a link about courses in your area, but it was right at the bottom of the page. I'm going to click on this link at the bottom of the page.

Learner clicks on link which takes him to learndirect website.

Learner: I presume from here I can find a local course.

Learner types 'dressmaking' into search box and fills out boxes about location, postcode, type of learning.

Learner: this has brought up a lot of courses in Leicester and in areas close by. This is what I expected from the original page rather than to have to come to this external site. But I did find it easy to work through the search box and options on the learndirect site.

Evaluator: Did you find this task difficult?

Learner: I didn't find it difficult. The first page was headed 'find a course in your area', and I was expecting to find something that would help me locate a course in my area. Instead the page was more about skills for life and online learning and stuff like that – but the page didn't do what it says, which is to help me find a course in my area.

Photo: Nick Hayes

Add functionality

Once users are satisfied with a version of the prototype it can be developed further and functionality can be added.

Functionality is added by ensuring that all the buttons and icons in the resource are working, for example all the hyperlinks are 'live' and any audio or video clips work when the users click on 'play'.

The fully functional version of the e-learning resource should also be tested for usability with learners and tutors who will be using it.

Evaluate the user interface

Heuristic evaluation is commonly used to evaluate the interfaces of websites for usability. It usually involves evaluators browsing through a website and evaluating the user interface against some usability guidelines (heuristics). This approach can be easily adapted to evaluate the user interfaces of your e-learning resources.

Evaluating the user interface

Prepare
Recruit between three and five potential users who will act as the evaluators. Ensure they are familiar with the usability guidelines listed on pages 30–31 of this book.

Evaluate
Ask each of the evaluators to work on their own through the e-learning resource and to use the usability guidelines as a checklist to identify potential usability problems. They should make a note of any problems they come across and indicate which of the usability guidelines it violates. See the example problem sheet on page 40.

Analyse findings
After each of the individual evaluations has been carried out, the group should meet and identify collectively how severe each of the problems are. One way of doing this is to rate each of the problems identified on a scale of 1–3:

1   is a cosmetic problem, i.e. change colour or font;
2   is a minor problem, e.g. missing link;
3   is a major problem, e.g. no feedback given on activities or tasks
    carried out by learners.

Identify solution
The problems that received the high severity ratings should be addressed and the evaluators should work with the designer(s) to decide on the changes to be made to the interface.

Example of a problem sheet filled out by a user evaluating the interface of the e-learning resource against usability principles.

Usability principles	Problem(s) identified
Keep learners informed	I clicked on the 'play' button and nothing happened. I was given no feedback on how long I should continue waiting.
Use plain language	1. Not sure what the 'status' link referred to. 2. A glossary would have been useful
Provide learners with control and freedom	Couldn't move from one lesson to the next without going via homepage.
Be consistent in the design and layout	1. Not all of the links were underlined – there was no consistency between what was a link and what wasn't. 2. There is no back button
Prevent learners from making errors	The response boxes are too close together. It is easy to click on the wrong box by mistake
Make use of recognition rather than recall	None
Ensure flexibility and efficiency of use	You cannot stop in the middle of a lesson without ending the session.
Use minimalist design	The response boxes are too small. It was difficult to see what I was typing in the box.
Help learners to recognise, diagnose, and recover from errors	There were no error messages when I clicked outside of the picture.
Provide help and documentation	There is no help or documentation

You can use co-operative evaluation to evaluate the fully functional version of the resource; however, it may not provide as much feedback as a heuristic evaluation will about important aspects of the interface with your resource, such as navigation and the use of colours and fonts.

Tutors and learners may also need some time to learn how to use the heuristic evaluation method, but with practice they will become more confident and competent in carrying them out.

8

Implementing e-learning resources

The final stage of the user-centred model is implementation, at which point the e-learning resources are made available to learners and tutors.

This chapter will provide an overview of the issues that you need to be aware of before, during and after e-learning resources have been implemented.

Access to e-learning resources

(i) Local network

If an e-learning resource is going to be delivered through an organisation's network, then you need to ensure that you have permission to upload it onto the network.

Also, it is useful to have two copies of the e-learning resource. One on the network, which your learners and tutors can access, and another on a 'test' server, where you can make any changes to the e-learning resource without causing any disruption to learners.

(ii) CD-ROM

If you intend to deliver your e-learning resource using CD-ROMs then ensure that you make enough copies to distribute out to your learners and tutors. Remember to allow for the time and resources that will be needed to copy and distribute the CD-ROMs.

Some of your learners and tutors may not be familiar with uploading a CD-ROM, so ensure that there are printed instructions with the disk on how to upload the resource on to a computer.

Finally, do not assume that all the computers at your learning centres will have a CD drive – check beforehand.

(iii) World Wide Web

If your e-learning resources are going to be delivered through a website then you need to ensure they are designed to be viewed using any browser. Do not assume that all your learners will be using the latest version of Internet Explorer, with all the plug-ins and programs that you may require them to have for your website. Also, ensure that your website can still be viewed correctly if the learner changes the text size or screen settings on their browser.

Finally, remember that your learners may be accessing the website using a dial-up connection and therefore will have difficulty downloading large files or images.

(iv) Learning platform

If you decide to deliver your e-learning resources using a learning platform then you may need to consider providing your learners with induction to both the course materials and the learning environment.

Also, a learning platform will have lots of materials from other courses and tutors: to avoid any confusion for your learners ensure that the resources are clearly labelled and where appropriate should be meta-tagged.

Training and support for tutors

Before tutors use the e-learning resources with their learners they will need to feel confident about using the resources themselves. Tutors may require some technical training and support in how to use the e-learning resources, as well as having some understanding of how to integrate the materials into their lessons. Workshops or one-to-one sessions with tutors to go through the e-learning resource and discuss how it can be used are often a useful start.

Also, try to ensure that tutors have access to some form of technical support should they have any problems using the resource.

Training and support for learners

Learners who are not familiar with ICT may need additional training before they are able to use your e-learning resources. For example, you may need to provide training on the use of a mouse or uploading CD-ROMs. If learners are using e-learning resources on their home computers then you need to ensure that they have any plug-ins required for the resource to work (e.g. *Flash*, *Media Player*). It is also helpful to provide them with a brief user guide to assist with any problems they may have with using the resource on their own.

Evaluating the e-learning resource

At the implementation stage, evaluations focus on how the resource is received by the tutors and the learners. At the end of the course, evaluations should be carried out to assess whether the resource has helped or hindered the learners in achieving the learning objectives of the course. However, you could continue to carry out ongoing evaluations with your users by observing your learners and tutors as they work with the e-learning resources and noting any problems or difficulties they have. Also, speak to your learners and tutors to find out what improvements can be made to existing resources and to elicit views and ideas for future resources.

Raising awareness of the e-learning resource

Although your e-learning resource may have been designed to be used in a particular curriculum area or with a specific group of learners, it is important that as many tutors and learners in your organisation are aware of the resource. You may find that your resource can be re-purposed by tutors in other curriculum areas. By working with tutors across curriculum areas you may be able to share ideas and experiences to produce better e-learning resources for your learners.

Numeracy Resources – Remploy, Sheffield

Graham Wroe, a basic skills tutor and a trained e-guide, has created a number of numeracy e-learning resources. The resources are hosted on his website and provide quizzes and activities for Entry Level 1 right through to Level 2 numeracy exercises. The exercises and activities were initially intended for learners at Remploy in Sheffield, but could easily be used by other numeracy tutors or learners.

Graham created these simple exercises using Hot Potato software and illustrated them with images from a typical working day at Remploy. He applied an iterative process to develop resources which would be used by the learners at Remploy.

This is still very much work in progress. I have asked for comments from the learners at Remploy and I am continuing to improve and add to the resource

Graham Wroe

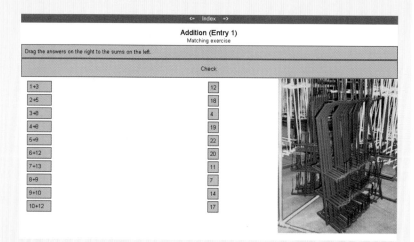

Example of Entry Level 1 Exercise
www.Grahamwroe.dsl.pipex.com/numeracy

9

Summary

The creation of e-learning resources using a user-centred design approach typically requires tutors to:

> Identify potential learners and their learning needs.

> Identify the current ICT skills of your learners.

> Identify the level of ICT skills and knowledge of the tutors who will be delivering and designing the e-learning resources.

> Investigate the environment in which the learning will be delivered (i.e. the level of hardware and connectivity available in these locations).

> Calculate the cost implications of designing and developing the e-learning resource.

> Identify learning objectives for the course and decide on the learning activities/ content you want the resource to cover.

> Design prototypes of the e-learning and test with potential users. Repeat this process until you are satisfied that the prototype meets the needs of your users.

> Develop a fully functional version of the e-learning resource using appropriate design tools.

> Implement your e-learning resource and evaluate the final product with the learners and tutors.

> Ensure that your tutors and learners are provided with training and support to enable them to use the e-learning resources.

> Keep a record of all the processes and the results of any evaluations for future developments to the resource.

Following a user-centred methodology will ensure that the design of e-learning resources is driven by users' needs and not by the technology. It will also addresses issues of quality, usability and evaluation by ensuring that the users of the product (i.e. learners and tutors) are considered at each stage of the design and development cycle.

10

Glossary of terms

ACL
Adult and Community Learning.

authoring tools
Software that help developers create e-learning resources. Authoring tools reduce the amount of programming expertise required in order to be productive. Some authoring tools use visual symbols and icons in flowcharts, or a slide-show environment to make programming easier.

co-operative evaluation
Also known as 'think aloud', this is a method for evaluating e-learning resources in which users complete set tasks whilst being observed by the designer, the users possibly giving a running commentary on what they are thinking about as they use the resource. The designer sets tasks and then observes the user's problems in operating the system under test. The technique is designed to identify problems with early prototypes and to assist in the process of refining designs.

e-learning
The use of information and communications technology to support, enhance or deliver learning.

heuristic evaluation
An evaluation method where a design is examined independently by multiple evaluators. They evaluate the product for instances in which certain heuristics or usability guidelines are violated.

Hot Potatoes

The *Hot Potatoes* suite of software includes six applications, enabling the creation of interactive multiple-choice, short-answer, jumbled-sentence, crossword, matching/ordering and gap-fill exercises for the World Wide Web. *Hot Potatoes* is not freeware, but it is free of charge for those working for publicly-funded non-profit-making educational institutions, who make their pages available on the World Wide Web.

ICT (Information and Communication Technology)

Any modern digital method of collecting, processing and communicating information of any kind, for example, text, graphics, sound, image or video. The term ICT does not refer to any single technology but encompasses all aspects such as computer based technology, telecommunications, digital photography, broadcasting etc.

iterative

In e-learning resource development, iterative is used to describe a planning and development process where a resource is developed in small sections called iterations. Each iteration is tested and evaluated by the developers and potential end-users. Insights gained from the evaluation of iteration are used to determine the next step in development.

learning platform

A single online location at which course resources can be made available to learners. These resources can include course materials, communications tools such as email and conferencing, and a storage area for learners' work. Learning Platforms can be provided using a range of software/hardware solutions including, an academic intranet/extranet, software sold as a Virtual Learning Environment (VLE) as well as a range of other software solutions.

Metatag

A metatag can be attached to each individual page on the e-learning resource to provide information such as the title, description, and keywords about the content of the page. The information contained in metatags can be used by search engines to build their indexes.

plug-ins

Small pieces of software that allow your browser to display/execute additional files. Popular plug-ins enable your browser to display animation, play audio, video, etc.

re-purposed

To reuse content by revising or restructuring it for a different purpose than it was originally intended or in a different way.

Webquest

An inquiry-oriented activity in which some or all of the information that learners interact with comes from resources on the Internet.

Further Information

General

B Powell and G Minshull, 2004, *Choosing and using a learning platform in Adult and Community Learning,* NIACE (ICT team).

A Clarke and C Hesse, 2004, *Online Resources in the Classroom*, NIACE.

Designing e-learning resources

BECTA, 2004, *Paving the Way to Excellence: Standards for High Quality Content from the NLN*, BECTA.

R Gagné, 1987, *The Conditions of Learning,* Holt, Reinhart, and Winston.

D J Mayhew, 1999, *The Usability Engineering Lifecycle: A Practitioner's Handbook for User Interface Design,* Morgan Kaufmann.

J Nielsen, 1994, *Usability Engineering,* Morgan Kaufmann.

D A Norman,1988, *The Design of Everyday Things*, MIT Press.

Evaluation and usability testing

J S Dumas, J C Redish, 1999, *A Practical Guide to Usability Testing,* Intellect, Ltd (UK).

S King, 2000, *Don't Make Me Think – A Common Sense Approach To Web Usability*, Que.

A Monk, P Wright, J Haber, and L Davenport, 1993, *Improving your human–computer interface: A practical technique*, Prentice Hall.

M Pearrow, 2000, *Web Site Usability Handbook*, Charles River Media.

J Rubin, 1994, *Handbook of Usability Testing: How to Plan, Design, and Conduct Effective Tests,* Wiley.

C Snyder, 2003, *Paper Prototyping: The Fast and Easy Way to Design and Refine User Interfaces*, Morgan Kaufmann.

Accessibility

M Paciello, 2000, *Web Accessibility for People with Disabilities*, CMP Books.

J Slatin and S Rush *Maximum Accessibility – Making your website usable for everyone*, 2002, Addison-Wesley.

Useful websites

www.accessiblenet.org
AccessibleNet.org is an independent, online directory of links and resources about Web accessibility.

www.coursegenie.com
The course genie homepage.

www.eduserv.org.uk/chest
Eduserv Chest is a not-for-profit Information and Communications Technology Service Provider to education and the public sector. Offering software, data and courseware negotiation services, access management systems and online information solutions

www.e-learningcentre.co.uk
The e-Learning Centre has a large collection links to e-learning resources focusing on e-learning in the workplace, for professional development and in further and higher education.

www.microsoft.com/enable/guides
Microsoft provides some useful guides and links to step-by-step tutorials for accessibility features that are helpful for specific types of conditions.

www.rnib.org.uk
The Royal National Institute of the Blind has a software accessibility page, a good resource for anyone concerned with creating and purchasing accessible software and systems.

www.rsc-northwest.ac.uk/accessibility
This Regional Support Centre site provides some useful links and resources on accessibility.

http://tip.psychology.org/theories
The Theory into Practice (TIP) website is a good online resource for teaching and learning models.

www.useit.com
Jakob Nielsen's homepage, which includes some very useful information and advice on usability and evaluations.

http://web.uvic.ca/hrd/halfbaked
The *Hot Potatoes* website, where you can download the software and get information and advice on how to use it.